John Cyril Francis

Three Months' Leave in Somali Land

Being the Diaries of the Late Captain J. C. Francis

John Cyril Francis

Three Months' Leave in Somali Land
Being the Diaries of the Late Captain J. C. Francis

ISBN/EAN: 9783337080143

Printed in Europe, USA, Canada, Australia, Japan

Cover: Foto ©ninafisch / pixelio.de

More available books at **www.hansebooks.com**

THREE MONTHS' LEAVE

IN

SOMALI LAND.

Being the Diaries of the late

CAPTAIN J. C. FRANCIS,

PUBLISHED AFTER HIS DEATH.

LONDON:
R. H. PORTER, 18, PRINCES STREET, CAVENDISH SQUARE, W.

1895.

PREFACE.

The following diaries of the late Captain Francis' shooting trip in Somali Land have been printed for private circulation, at the request of a large number of his friends. They are taken from small pocket books, written in pencil only, and are almost entirely in his own words, but the writing having been in some places much rubbed, it has been difficult to be certain of the spelling of places.

Captain Francis left Berbera on January 1, 1894, and went due south, 300 miles, on a route called "James's route," which had not been travelled by white men since an exploring party under James went there in 1885. They reported thirteen days without water. After leaving the last water about four days from Berbera, Captain Francis took nine days' supply of it on camels and reached water on the morning of the eighth day. He describes it in a letter home as "a very hard country to work; plenty of lion and rhino, but no antelope to speak of. Dense thorn-bush and dense grass high overhead. It was very hard and very disappointing work, continually disturbing your beasts within a few yards and seeing nothing. You could not force your way through the jungle without noise, and they let you come pretty close and then slipped away."

It must be borne in mind by the readers of these diaries that they are only rough jottings of sport, and perhaps were not intended to be printed, but they will no doubt be valued for the sake of one who, during his short life, had made so many sincere friends.

K. M. A.

Sussex, 1894.

THREE MONTHS' LEAVE IN SOMALI LAND.

DIARY.

1893.

DECEMBER 24TH.—Left Aden at 6 p.m. Rough passage in *Tuna*, a small 80-ton steamer. Ill (*bahut sick!*).

25TH.—Arrived at Jibouti at 11.30 a.m. French port. All right again to-day.

26TH.—Left Jibouti; arrived Zaila 1.30 a.m.

27TH.—Left Zaila 1 p.m.; arrived Berbereh 6 a.m.

28TH, THURSDAY.—Bought camels and stores, and engaged men. Four camels.

29TH, FRIDAY.—Went out for a shoot in afternoon with Vandeleur. Had one shot at *gazella naso*, 130 yards, with 303 (walking), three-quarters away. Hit him in centre of stomach near side, passed out breaking shoulder off side. Jeffery bullet. Hole of exit about 12-bore size. Buck ran about thirty yards and died. Horns, 12 in. Davis left in morning. Eleven camels.

30TH, SATURDAY.— Nothing except arrangements. Am waiting for 10-bore.

31ST, SUNDAY.—All camels (twenty-two), &c., ready. Shall start to-morrow.

1894.

1ST JANUARY, MONDAY.—Went as far as Chefto, about eleven miles. Breakfasted there, and on in afternoon. Camped at sunset about twenty miles from Berbereh. No water. Had several shots at *gazella naso*. Missed one at 150 yards; two at about 130 yards; one at about 120 yards. Also missed another at 120 yards, who stood again at about 250 yards. Shot entered just behind off shoulder. *Gazella* walked slowly on for about 100 yards and lay down; finished him with shot through neck, close, forty yards. Saw many *dik-dik* (very small antelope). One herd of *gerenouk* (G. walleri); could not get near these. Used 303.

2ND JANUARY.—Started at 5.30. Shot at *dik-*

dik at about eighty yards (303); bullet passed straight through, making large hole far side. Shot a small bustard at sixty yards (303). Missed two shots at big bustard at about 130 yards. One shot grazed and brought out feathers. Stopped at Hámás for breakfast, thirty-two miles. Saw many *dik-dik*. Walked to Leferug, forty miles. Plenty water, but very sandy. Alas! have forgotten filter.

3RD JANUARY, WEDNESDAY.—Marched to Mandéra, forty-eight miles. Had a long shot at a *gazella*, about 180 yards, with 303; grazed him underneath, for I heard bullet strike, and he jumped straight up when hit. He went off for a long way, going strong; did not follow, as I found only a few drops of blood on track. Walked for about seven hours in the lesser *koodoo* jungle round Mandéra. Saw many does and two small bucks. Caught just a glimpse of the horns of a good buck as he went off; did not fire because of bushes, as I was using 500 with light bullet. Towards evening came across another buck, also going through bush; could only see horns; fired through bushes; bullet stopped and broken up by branches; no blood. Davis shot here

for three days last week, and killed five bucks,
hence the rest are few and wary. Met eight
men stalking through the jungle covered with
weapons. They held up a spear, so I and Jàma
advanced to talk to them. They were Esa
Moosa, tracking a man of the Habr Unis, who
had killed one of their men in the morning.
(N.B.—Jàma is Habr Unis.)

4TH, THURSDAY.—Started at 7 a.m. Walked
the lower slopes of Gan Libah till 11.30. Saw
one antelope (*Ālēkāt klipspringer*) at 9 a.m., eighty
yards, 303. Jeffery bullet. Hit behind near
shoulder, passed out of throat; dropped in his
tracks. At about 11.30 breakfasted. At 12.30
saw big *koodoo* 300 yards off going hard; he had
been lying to leeward of my line, and was thus
alarmed; followed his tracks. At about two
o'clock came on big *koodoo* and doe, about 150
yards, vanishing round corner. Had a snap shot.
Jàma wrung his hands in great grief; said I had
missed; presently saw doe go up opposite slope
alone; ran down to where he was when I fired;
saw *koodoo* standing below me about 100 yards;
head and withers hidden by bush; fired into the
middle of his back; dropped in his tracks

with broken back; had to give him a finisher before Jāma could cut his throat. First bullet hit stomach far back; second, spine; third, between withers (behind), 500, ex. hollow bullet. Was lucky to stop him at first shot. Magnificent beast, bigger than *sambur.* Head, 34 in. straight; 53 in. round curves. Got home at 4.30. Very hard day; stiff going. Quite satisfied with my shooting to-day. Sending back Murad and *koodoo* head to Abud.

5TH, FRIDAY.—Went out in morning along hills towards new camping ground on the plateau. Saw another *ălĕkūt* (antelope) standing on a rock at about 200 yards against sky line. As he is a smaller beast than a chink it was a hard shot. Lay down, rested on a rock and put up 200 yards sight, 303. Antelope dropped to shot, hit close behind, near shoulder, bullet (Jeffery), coming out of back of stomach offside. At about 10 a.m. came on big *koodoo* standing in shade of bush, tail on, seventy yards; first bullet just grazed stern; *koodoo* went about fifteen yards, stood side on, hit him on near shoulder, dropped to shot, 500 ex. hollow bullet. A *grand* beast sixteen hands and over. Head 39 in. straight, 48 in. round curves, 32½ in. between tips. A much grander looking head than yesterday's, though measurement round curves is not so good. Davis' two heads were 32 in. and 37 in., both considered good, 37 in. supposed to be Somaliland record, if so I have capped it easily. My camel men had practice with their Sniders this afternoon and enjoyed it immensely. They shoot fairly well and are awfully keen. The two antelope I have shot are *Klipspringer*. Name of this place Asa; have arrived in Habr Unis country. No "water-wong" here, but many ticks.

6TH, SATURDAY.—Marched to Ädălĕh, seven miles, last water before Haridigil. Had a shot at gazelle, 120 yards, 303 (Jeffery); hit in centre of shoulder, passed out of off shoulder, breaking it, exit hole 12-bore size. Gazelle dropped in tracks. Went out round Ädălĕh after breakfast; took out some Tweedie bullets and rifleite to try. Had two shots at *dik-dik* about 90 to 100 yards, went over both. Had a long shot 150 yards at least (I think further but I did not pace it), at *gerenouk* standing facing; bullet grazed right side, entered front of thigh, and passed out at back of it; he ran about fifty yards, stood, took full sight 200, went over, *gerenouk* moved not (thanks to smokeless powder he did not know where I was), fired again, fine sight, just cut along bottom of stomach, skin wound only, *gerenouk* vanished. Plenty of blood. He only went about 300 yards and lay down, could not get up when I got near, gave him a finisher through both shoulders. The Tweedie bullet and rifleite makes the most fearful wounds. The 303 is a far more powerful weapon than I believed. *Gerenouk's* head 14 in. Sultan Nur, the boss of this part came to see me, drank tea, &c., and told me that I ought to take more camels for water across the Haud. Shall hire two from here. Saw lots of *gerenouk* to-day, they are the hardest antelope to get near, I know. Their enormous long necks enable them to see over bushes well. They run through the bush with the head down and long neck straight out; look very comic moving. They are a little bigger than black buck, but much longer in leg and neck. If you crossed a very small camel and a *chinkard* and reared the offspring on gin to keep it small, you might grow a *gerenouk*.

7TH, SUNDAY.—Went out after breakfast. Sultan Nur came to see me again before breakfast; gave him a "tobe," a packet of tea and dates for his men. First things I saw on the Haud were two wart-hog boars, distance 200 yards, ground very open. Allowed too much for movement (they were walking); cut the throat of No. 1 boar (Tweedie 303); dropped in his tracks, kicking. The other walked all round with his tail straight up on end, wondering what had happened to his pal. First shot passed over him, second got him through both shoulders (Tweedie 303) and he dropped. Went up to first, who was apparently dying, went on to the second, who was dead when I arrived, both shoulders broken. First pig was now sitting up on his forelegs. On my going up to finish him he galloped off; hit him in the left thigh as he was going away; he went a few yards and lay down under a bush, was not dead when I got up, so I finished him with another shot. Next thing I saw was an *aoul* (*sœmeringii*). Got up to 150 yards and missed him, fired too low; he stood again about 300 yards, fired two more shots, one of which I heard hit. Followed him for a long way, firing occasional shots at about 350 to 400 yards. He would let me get to nearly 300, and then go straight away directly I sat down to shoot.

The twelfth shot I had at him hit him fair behind, coming out of stomach (Jeffery 303); he went only a short distance and lay down. I got to 100 yards under cover of small bush, and shot him through both shoulders. Found both hind legs had been slightly hit, and a bullet hole sideways through one foreleg just below elbow, bone untouched. I had been firing too low all along. Hit him five times out of thirteen; head eighteen inches. Shot a hare sitting up 70 yards, 303. Got back to camp and found my 10-bore had come. Move on to-morrow. Habr Unis tried to steal a camel of mine this evening, two men. My camel men saw them making off with it, ran after them and shouted. They continued to drive the camel off, so my men fired three shots. No result, except that they left the camel and ran. Have been going bare-legged lately, legs fearfully burnt, I can hardly stand.

8TH. MONDAY.—Spent the morning in casting 10-bore bullets and loading 10-bore cartridges. Started on the march at 1 p.m. Arrived at

Oouoonoof 5.15 p.m., about twelve miles. Shot one *gerenouk* fourteen inches, thick horns, two shots 200 yards. First hit behind right shoulder, passing out in front of shoulder (Jeffery 303), broke shoulder only. Second hit left buttock, came out behind right shoulder. *Gerenouk* went about 300 yards and lay down. Shot small bustard (303 Jeffery) fifty yards. Had one shot at *aoul*, 400 yards sight, missed. One at another *aoul*, 300 yards sight, missed. Saw tracks of *oryx*. Found camel men had made my camp in an old zereba. Ground appeared to be mostly camel dung, with some sand below. Found after five minutes the soil was chiefly composed of ticks. Have been sitting with my feet upon the bed since I came in. Anointed feet and legs of bed with phenyle; hope to pass a night somehow. Do not care much about dining with my legs cocked up. I will make my own zerebas in future.

9TH, TUESDAY.—Started 5.40 a.m., marched till 10. Started again at 1.30 p.m., marched till 5.15. Shot very badly in the morning, was going through mimosa with a few open patches. Misjudged distance every time, as much as I under estimated them in the open plain, so much did I over estimate in cover. Missed three shots, at *aoul*—150, 200, 250 yards, I estimated, but went over every time. Missed two shots at an *oryx*, only one I saw—200, 250 yards, thus I estimated, went over both times. Had four shots at *aoul* in the afternoon, in more open ground, 200 yards sight each time. First, hit just behind shoulder, but too low, dropped. Second, miss—another buck. Third, shot another buck through both shoulders. Found first buck had got up and moved off, fired at him again, hit clean through both shoulders. Shooting in afternoon not so bad. Saw two big bustard, stalk failed, *mea culpa*. Saw crowds of *gerenuuk*. Came across tracks of many galloping horses. Ogaden made a raid into Habr Unis ten days ago, 800 horsemen. Looted about 400 camels. The Habr Unis pursued, but failed to recapture much. Five of their horses died from over-galloping. They captured eight horses and five men from the Ogaden, three of whom died. Two were at Syk when I passed through, waiting for ransom.

10th, Wednesday.—Started at 5.50 a.m. Open plain called Toyo. Stopped at 9.45 under six trees in middle of plain (Chalelo). Marched at

1.15 till 5 p.m., crossed open plain and arrived in thin bush jungle. Saw plenty *oryx*. Absolutely unapproachable in open, fired three shots 500 yards sight, one shot 400 yards, no result. Shot one big bustard 120 yards, missed one about same distance. My guide tells me this evening that we *may* get water six days from here; probably shall get none for nine days. Must march all I know, for I have only seven days' water. The guide lied about distance up till now. He may be lying still. Saw lion pugs about two days old.

11TH, THURSDAY.—Started 4.10 a.m., marched till 10.10 a.m., again from 1.55 p.m. till 5.10 p.m., all the way through bush and grass jungle; saw lion pugs several times, none very fresh. Saw ostrich pugs three times. Saw two *oryx*, lost the chance by taking it a bit too easy; the one I was going to fire at dodged away through the bush as I raised the rifle.

12TH, FRIDAY.—Started a bit late, about 4.45 a.m., marched till 10.15 through bush jungle. Saw several lion pugs about, none fresh. Cafala (travelling party) from Ogaden passed us. Say there is a little water at Luckha, enough for men but not enough to give camels a square drink. Saw rhino pugs two days old. After first halt, march during afternoon through more open plain. Marched 1.50 till 5.10 p.m., and found an old zareba evidently not used except by stray cafalas; camped there; after 4 p.m. road took a more westerly direction (have been going south up to date). Saw Clarke's gazelle, one female Fired three long shots at *oryx* 400 yards (over I think) 500 yards moving, all misses, last two under. Came across two *oryx* in a bit of bush about 3.30, got up to 90 or 100 yards, shot at longest horns (or what seemed longest), first shot staggered, stopped still; second shot (only shoulder showing through bush) just in front of shoulder, miss; third shot on part of shoulder, dropped. The *oryx* had not yet made me out. The other was about 120 yards looking my way. Shot him in shoulder, but too low, I fancy. Stood again at 200 yards. Could not keep Jāma in; he is like a half-broke retriever, keen as mustard but too excitable, he ran towards the dropped one shouting, and frightened the other before I could get a second shot into him; tracked him some way, very little blood, bullet had evidently not passed through, had to give him up as he was going straight away from my route. Dead *oryx*, female, 31½ in. horns. I cannot tell bucks from does of this beast. Used Jeffery 303. First shot on dead *oryx* 1 ft. behind shoulder; one bullet passed out in front of opposite shoulder, other stayed in body; did not assist at the cutting up, so am not sure of the nature of wounds.

13TH, SATURDAY.— Started at 3.55 a.m.; marched till 10 a.m. Saw fresh lion pugs about 8 a.m., followed and lost in bad ground. Saw fresh rhino pugs at 10 a.m., followed into dense bush where the pugs formed a kind of maze; had not time nor strength in me to work out the puzzle. Walked in and out of the thick bit, hoping to put him up and give him a dose of 10-bore as he flapped off; no luck. Character (Darur) of country changed at 8.30 a.m., stony, slightly undulating, bigger mimosa trees. Guinea-fowl in hundreds, and dried up tanks instead of the now monotonous sand bush and grass of the Haud. Country here varies, bits of Haud, interspersed with bits of stone country, can get a view now and then, see some high ground in the distance. Afternoon march as usual two to five o'clock. Bad leg (forgot to mention I hurt left leg yesterday, tried to ride to ease it, but pony could not carry me, so walked, or rather limped along), getting better, does not hurt when I have once got warm in going, but I came out of the zereba very unsound in the morning.

14TH, SUNDAY.—Marched from 3.55 to 10 a.m., and again from 1.55 to 5.5; did not arrive at water. Guide swears it is only an hour's march further, but he has lied so often that I do not expect to reach it under three hours; however, he is going to take two men and go on to the water after dinner, and arrange with the men there for supply of gafila (caravan). Had two fruitless stalks after *oryx*, and one successful one. In the latter I was spotted at about 250 or 300 yards, fired standing, as the grass was high, miss, over I think; fired again, standing position, at a good 300 yards. Caught buck *oryx* on shoulder rather low. He kicked out behind and ran into some bush, found him dead 150 yards on. It was rather a good standing shot if not a fluke, horns thirty inches. Fired at an *aoul* 200 yards, went over, I think; fired again, same sight, when he was a bit further off, fell on both knees, got up and was going off slowly when I hit him behind again; heard the bullet crack on him plainly. He went off very slowly, looking very sick; as I was going after him I saw another buck with a *grand head* standing 200 yards; fired and he dropped; when Jāma went to cut his throat he ran off quite fresh. I followed him, sending the Midgan (low caste Somali) after the other; "lashings" of blood; he seemed to be hit high on shoulder, as he was covered with blood there. Followed him for about three-quarters of a mile by blood tracks, when he got up and went off from 300 yards ahead quite fresh; had to give him up as I was going straight away from my line. Midgan lost the other. Cannot understand the luck. I was using 303 with rifleite and Tweedie bullet.

15TH, MONDAY.—Found water at Lackhu, about one hour from where I camped at night, not much, but can give camels half a drink, pony and donkeys a full one, and fill up casks. Water in wells dug in the bed of dry banks. Ogaden came to see me, said that they could spare water to-day, as some of their braves were on a raid with their ponies. The said braves came back this evening, nine of them on ponies; they came to have a "buck" with the men in my camp; they had suffered no loss and their loot was twenty-two camels (I counted them), not a bad haul for a small party. They say there are two male lions here who have been robbing their zerebas regularly; mean to halt as long as water will let me. Tied up one donkey near their *karias* (native villages or encampments), one near my zereba. Shot a *dik-dik* ninety yards, 303 solid. Found no lion pugs.

16TH, TUESDAY.—Moved camp to *karias* about three miles west. No donkeys killed. Walked for hours morning and afternoon in good tracking ground and saw never a lion pug old or new. Hyæna rushed a flock of sheep just as I passed; of course, I thought it was a lion; much disgusted when I spotted the well-known front. Am among the Rer Harun Ogaden. Politics of this section, briefly; loot your neighbour when you can, and make as much out of a European who passes as you may. N.B., I am the first; God help the second. They *sell* water here. Talking of water there is a field for sport yet unfound by travellers in this land. The water contains game of every description. I swallowed a fine elephant this evening in my drink; had I had a gun and an emetic handy, I might have bolted him and shot him flying. Another chance lost! Shikar to-day, four shots at guinea-fowl with 303 between 60 and 120 yards. All misses. Leg getting very bad from constant walking, must lay up and give it a show to heal to-morrow.

16TH, TUESDAY.—Leg bad, lay up, sent men out in morning, no *khubber*. Marched 12.30 till 4.45 (rode), saw nothing but *dik-dik*, guinea-fowl, and such small game. Shot one bustard (small), 303, 15 yards.

17TH, WEDNESDAY.—Marched (rode) 4.45 a.m. to 7.30 a.m. to Redab Safar, where lions were reported. *Karia* gone. Men could find never a track around. Country gameless except for *dik-dik* (hundreds) guinea-fowl, &c.; high grass and dense bush. Marched 1.15 till 4.30, came on fresh tracks of goats; halted; sent men to look for *karia*, found three miles off. Report one lioness regularly living on them. Water said to be one very long march off. Shall halt here till

I kill her or give it up as hopeless. Can send my camels on to water easy. Shot two *dik-dik*, forty yards, missed one about same distance (over), 303.

18TH, THURSDAY.—Only *khubber* is that lioness tried to rush a herd of goats at about 6 p.m. yesterday, but was frightened off. Moved my camp to the biggest *karia*, from which she is reported to have taken a goat two nights ago. Could find no fresh pugs. Made a small zereba outside *karia*, sent off camels to Gagli, keeping two camels and five men with me. Have water now for three more days.

19TH, FRIDAY.—Found lioness pugs close to my zereba. Followed from 7.45 to 12.15, lost pugs in hard sand ground. Got back 2.30. Heard that about 2,000 Abyssinians camped last night one day's march west, and started this morning for Gogli. Must give up lioness and march all I know to try and get to my kit before them. If they loot my camels, the whole show is up, so consider it best to give up the chance of this lioness, though it looks good.

20TH, SATURDAY.—Marched from 4 p.m. to 7.15 p.m. yesterday. To-day from 5 a.m. till 10 a.m., and 1.30 p.m. till 5.45 p.m. Did a good twenty-eight miles to-day. Direction south till 3.15, when I got into hilly country, direction south-east. Camped in an old zereba. Thick jungle here, no open bits. Shot guinea-fowl, 303, 50 yards. Saw no game except two does of lesser *koodoo*. No sign of Abyssinians.

21st, Sunday.—Marched 5 a.m. till 7.30 a.m. Came on fresh pugs of rhino; ordered a halt and tracked from 7.30 till 11.30, mostly through grass over my head and dense thorn-bush; lost track, took a cast ahead through some very thick grass about shoulder high. Rush in the grass about sixty yards ahead, just saw a bit of the back of a red animal, for a second, took it for *oryx* from colour; did not fire. Found that I had lost a chance (and a very hard chance) at a rhino. Another of the illusions of my boyhood vanished. I thought the black rhino was black. He's not here; he's just a brick colour! The soil being dark red sand and there being no water, I ought to have expected the unwashed rhino. to be the colour of mother earth, but I didn't. Saw lots of rhino pugs on road. At Jugli at 5 p.m. found two of my camels waiting for me with water. Abyssinian alarm a fraud. It is only a small force sent to collect tribute. Gogli and my kit reported five hours' distance; shall stay here and shoot; people say there are lots of rhino. No lions, a few reported near Gogli, they can wait. Country alternate low hill and plain, trees bigger, bush in places almost impenetrable. Shot one *dik-dik*, missed one, 303. Tasted camel's milk for first time; it is excellent in my opinion.

22ND, MONDAY. — In morning went out on *khubber* of fresh lion pugs (pugs yesterday's); while looking in direction a lion had been heard roaring, two of my men spotted a rhino. Went with them, found her standing under a tree just outside thick grass cover, forty yards, quarter facing me. Fired with 10-bore at point of shoulder; rhino was off before smoke cleared. Tracked through high grass, found rhino dead about 130 yards on. Hit point of shoulder halfway up. Went on to look for more rhino; found none. Got back 1.30. Found two lions had killed a camel about one mile from camp, other direction. That ass Warsam let the Midgans go to get the meat. When I arrived camel was skinned and half cut up. No lions of course. Had to sit up. Made a small zereba. Jāma and I entered at 3 p.m. About 6.30 a lion stalked quietly out, and stood about ten yards, quarter facing, head turned to me. Got him on point of shoulder half-way up, 10-bore hollow bullet. Collapsed and died at once. Men came up on hearing shot, brought dinner and coat, decided to stay for other animal. Heard him coming as I was eating; he came about 7.15, and smelt the blood of the other lion; he was too far off to make certain, as it was nearly dark in the bush. He went away, came round behind us and spotted us I think; he remained around, calling occasionally till 11.30, when he went off, his call sounding fainter and fainter in the distance. Hard, hilly ground, no use trying for his tracks. Lion measured 9 ft. $2\frac{1}{2}$ in., hardly a sign of mane. Rhino. horns (female, but a big one), front $12\frac{3}{4}$ in. long, 16 in. circumference. Rear 7 in. long, 17 in. circumference. Jāma fooling with 12-bore has broken a striker, gun useless.

23RD, TUESDAY.—Did an off-day in the morning, looked after skins, &c. Took a stroll in the afternoon, came on rhino pugs (fresh) in two places, but could not find the rhino; very dense cover. Shot a partridge, 303 solid, in the evening.

24th, Wednesday.—A Somali said he knew a place where there were lots of rhino, said it was quite close, that we could go there, shoot a rhino or two and be back before 10 o'clock. Took no breakfast, started at 6.45, at 8.45 after two hours' hard walking Somali said we had not got half way. This meant nothing to eat till 4 p.m. at least, so I chucked it. Saw fresh rhino pugs on way back, tracked him for some way and lost him in hard ground. Missed a *dik-dik* with 303, in evening. Kit which I ordered to arrive here to-day has not turned up.

25th, Thursday.—Sent out men in two directions, and went for a short stroll with Ali; saw pugs of big rhino, but the evening's pugs, while following them came on five wild dogs, very dark, handsome skins, but I didn't fire because of the rhino. Could not find him, came back, and one of the local men said he knew where that rhino usually lay up; he went out and came back in an hour saying he had seen the rhino and alarmed him in a very thick bit of cover. Went out with Jāma, and crawled through the most awful bit of thick bush I have ever seen. After about 400 yards of tracking, heard rhino snort and go off about twenty yards ahead. Could see nothing, after about another 400 yards, same thing; this time bush a little more open. I ran forward and just had a snap shot at his stern about forty yards ahead. Bullet hit a 3 in. branch and was I think deflected, for height and direction were correct; followed for some time, no blood, and rhino going like blazes for the West of Africa; expect he is going still. Kit arrived, have now tent, table, and chair, was getting tired of living under a bush. Water here very brackish, everything cooked with it is beastly. Abdullah brings *khubba* of lion one day's march; shall go day after to-morrow.

26TH, FRIDAY.—Went out in morning with Jāma and Ali; saw fresh rhino pugs, lost in hard ground after a long track. Searched a bit of dense cover on hill top towards which tracks lead; nothing; not satisfied; went out again at 12.45, searched the whole hill top, could find no rhino, cover very dense, very hard work getting through it, took a round beyond the hill but could find no tracks.

27th, Saturday. — Moved to Adáleh about fourteen miles south, then five miles southeast. There are reported two lions here. Abdullah came to inspect and reported water plentiful and good. It is very scarce, so much so that I can hardly get them to sell me any, and it is the worst water I have ever seen, not very brackish but black as ink, with an indescribable stench, and a thick blue scum on it. Fired one shot at a *dik-dik*, grazed his back and dropped him, but he got off into the bush when Ali went to "haltal" him (cut his throat). These people here have mostly never seen a European. I am like a circus elephant in a country village, and am getting sick of being crowded round and inspected all day long. I think gate-money for entrance into my zereba would be profitable. The head-men all come with the same complaint—want my protection against Abyssinians. I am not going to try that game; there are 1,100 of them in a big zereba two days off. They say they want to come and see me. There is no danger to a

European from the Abyssinians. Abdullah says if they come, they will present me with sheep and cows. Three Abyssinians are reported to have been killed by the Somalis. They will have to pay heavily for them.

28TH, SUNDAY.—To Théin, three miles south. Could find no pugs. Tied up donkey at water where lions are said to drink; no kill. Great difficulty in getting water, and that of the very worst description. A camel has fallen into the only large well here, and these folk were too lazy to pull it out; water of course undrinkable there.

29TH, MONDAY.—Went for the usual stroll, saw nothing. Ali and Hassan saw pugs of lion two days old. Donkey again. No kill.

30TH, TUESDAY.—Went out towards where the pugs were seen, those of one lion very big. Got back at 12.15, found a man from Dhorké waiting. Ali has been over there; people say that lions have worried around their zereba the last two nights. Went to Dhorké in evening; sat up over tied up donkey; no lions; left donkey there with orders to tie up nightly. Leopard visited camp last night.

31ST, WEDNESDAY.—Went out after *dik-dik* with

303 solid. First shot at partridge walking, fifteen yards. Miss. Shot seven *dik-dik* one after the other without a miss, at distances from forty to ninety yards, all shots fired in standing position. One wounded *dik-dik* got into grass and was lost, back broken apparently. Eighth shot fired sitting position, kill, 100 yards. Ninth shot miss, standing, thirty yards; *dik-dik* moved as I fired. *Very* straight powder to-day, *dik-dik* all of the long-nosed kind called by Somalis "*ghusi*." A man at 6 p.m. said lions caught two cows last night in a *karia* three miles beyond Dhorké; too late to do anything. Somalis eat one cow, the other still alive.

1st FEBRUARY, THURSDAY.—A man came in from Dhorké at 6 a.m. Said lions had been round their zereba at night but had not killed my donkey. Could not understand it till I got there (8.45), when I found that they had been too lazy to tie up the donkey, though the spot was only 100 yards from their fence. They are a God-forsaken, thriftless race and the greatest liars on earth. Tracked the lions from 8.45 a.m. to 11.15. Two large males I should say. Tracks led into a dense piece of bush and grass about 100 yards square. Grass as high as my head and thick bush. Crept through it all except one bit about forty yards square where the wait-a-bit was too thick to get through except on all fours. Could find no tracks the other side so determined to fire it.

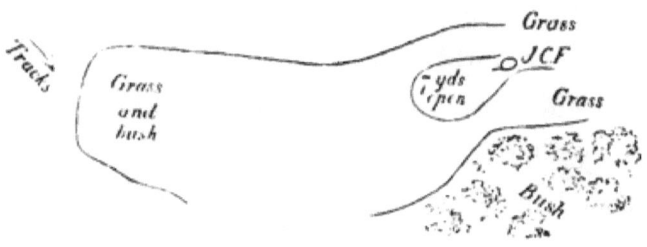

That was the position, not a nice one, with two lively lions and a fire behind them. I would not have stood there for a tiger. The furthest I could see was seven yards, on one side the grass came up to me, on the other side there was a path a yard wide. It was very exciting, but the lions were not there! Found tracks afterwards further on, and lost them where the sand was hard and the bush dense. Camels from Théin feeding all round this; expect they will kill or follow camels back to Théin to-night. Shall have one donkey tied up outside *karia*.

2ND FEBRUARY, FRIDAY.—Lions killed my donkey at *karia* last night. I expected to find them lying up close, as they eat a lot. Tracks, one large male, one female. Followed from 6.15 till 11, when tracks took us to my old camping ground at Adāleh. Here men at well said lions had entered their *karia* and killed a cow at 3 a.m., and were driven off from it. Found tracks utterly blotted out by cattle, &c.; could make nothing of it. Got back to camp 1 p.m., badly hungry, as I took no breakfast. Shall sit up over dead donkey, but it does not look as if the lions meant to come back.

3RD FEBRUARY, SATURDAY.—No lions at night. My pet horseman from Dhorké was coming in to give me khubber that lions had been round his *karia* again last night, when, at about 5.30 a.m., he met a lion on the road. He reached me just before 6 a.m., had a big drink of milk and went off at once; found tracks where he had evidently turned the lion. Ground bad for tracking. After much trouble took his tracks into a dense bit about

300 yards away, worked it carefully through and found tracks going into another large, dense bit of thorn and grass. Took the track with much difficulty into the very thickest of it. Lion got up *within* five yards of me, in grass eight feet high, and though I could see the grass move, &c., I could not see a hair of the beast. Fired the bit, I sitting ahead on the look out. Horseman seeing the fire and hearing my men (two only) shouting came and joined in, but exactly in the direction I wanted quiet, viz., behind me. I could not get him away by frantic signals; he paraded up and down about thirty yards behind me. Lion broke back through unburnt bit on the right, and went into a very long bit of dense cover, too large to fire, and too dense to follow a possibly angry lion into. I, at least, concluded it not good enough; odds too much with the lion. My people want me to move to Dhorké, shall start this evening.

Abyssinians at *karia*, two miles off, went to see them. They have the boss of this section of the Ogaden with them, who tells me that he has arranged with the Abyssinians to give them so much from each *karia*, so I did not interfere. Seven Abyssinians, armed with Remingtons, say they want to come to my camp and see me. Moved to Dhorké.

4TH FEBRUARY, SUNDAY.—Heard lion calling last night, but going off south from here; afraid fire has sent him off. No tracks to-day. Hear that Lord Delamere and party are expected here day after to-morrow on their way to the Webi; they have come through Dholbanta.

5TH FEBRUARY.—No tracks. Went to look for *oryx* on a bit of open two miles off; saw tracks, but no *oryx*. Baladier from Abyssinian camp came in, is taking *gafila* to Berbera shortly; sent letters by him.

6TH, TUESDAY.—Went for a stroll in morning; met a man from Théin, who said a lion had taken a sheep from their *karia* at night; went at once to get tracks before cattle were out. Found track led into a thick bit about a mile off. Tracks big male lion. Tracks of two lions leading out, followed till about 3 p.m.; lost tracks in big dense bit of jungle about one and a half miles south-east of Théin.

7TH, WEDNESDAY.—Heard that about two hours after I left, lions killed a camel in the dense bit. Went in morning, found tracks of big male lion,

could do nothing with him in that place, made
zereba to sit up at night; lion at about 8.30
came suddenly round corner of my zereba, so
close to the shooting hole that I could have
touched him; he was off with a roar before I
could raise gun, and stood about eight yards off
growling loudly. I could not make him out as
he had a dense bush for background. Jāma
begged me to shoot or he would go, so I fired at
the noise; lion roared loudly at the shot and
after about a second galloped off. Miss, I
thought. Nothing more except a hyæna till
morning.

8th, Thursday.—Took up tracks at 5.45, found
blood, but no great quantity, all legs sound,
blood high up where he brushed through grass;
grazed neck or top of shoulder, I think. After
about a mile, put up lion in cover about fifteen
yards ahead, could not see him, went round the
patch, no tracks out, as it was partly dense, high
grass, and partly thick bush. Ordered it to be
burnt, I sitting ahead. Fire soon went out,
nothing came. Jāma came and said there was
a thick bit of bush unburnt. After much
persuasion he got me to go in. I did not like

it. Crawling on hands and knees through tunnels in the bush, you could see a bit on both sides and branches too low for a lion to come at you except slowly, so it was not quite so bad as it looked. Went through it twice, back and forward, saw nothing but tracks with wet blood. Found on coming out that the lion had left, must have sneaked out when we were in the bush. Followed for another mile and lost tracks (no blood) in bad ground at 2 p.m. near the big dense bit. Gave it up. Had no dinner sent me last night, only two cups of milk this morning, no water all day for self and men. I was thoroughly done and very angry with the people in camp for sending nothing; gave up and came back, reached camp 5 p.m.

9TH, FRIDAY.—Went after lion again. Found his fresh pugs in thick low bush, not much grass, fair tracking. Followed till 11.15, putting him up three or four times without seeing him; breakfast, followed again till 1 p.m. Rested an hour and followed again till 3 p.m., lion keeping carefully out of sight all the time. Very hard going, as it was continual stooping under bush. This patch of bush about three square miles, and as lion kept going in a circle, no hope of getting him out of it; gave him up as I saw no chance of his giving me a shot. N.B.—A wounded lion, unless cornered, does not seem keen on fighting, and this was a big male. Saw very little blood to-day. Left camp at 5.50 a.m. Got back at 4.40 p.m.

10TH, SATURDAY.—Marched west five and a quarter hours, roughly fifteen miles. Camels lightly laden went fast. Saw fresh tracks of lioness, led back to Adaleh and thence struck off in direction of big jungle at Théin. Did not follow further. She is the mate of the wounded one. Shot at *dik-dik* on march. First six shots missed four *dik-dik*, one bustard (small), wounded and lost one *dik-dik*, next six shots killed four *dik-dik*, one bustard (small), one hare. Lord Delamere's party went this road to the Webi yesterday. Small well at this place named Bāli Gābāli.

11TH, SUNDAY.—Marched five hours north-west, came across some bush jungle with tracks of lesser *koodoo*, saw three does and one buck, but could not get a shot. Ordered camp, as I want to get a head of this species. Kāriä one and a half miles off say lion visits occasionally. Shot four *dik-dik*, wounded and lost one ten yards. Fired four shots at one *dik-dik* about fifty yards off; he stood absolutely still all the time, till the fourth shot cut him over, I standing and firing in full view of him!!!

12TH, MONDAY.—Elhär, spent all the morning after *koodoo*; saw only does, and few of them. There was a lot of low thorn-bush about shoulder high, which was hard and painful to get through, and the thorns scraping against one's clothes alarmed the *koodoo* before you saw them. The does I saw were in an open bit; saw fresh tracks of *oryx*. Left Elhär at 1.45, marched till 5 p.m., general direction north-west, shot two *dik-dik*, two cartridges. Country more open, saw *gerenook*, and tracks of *oryx*.

13TH, TUESDAY.—Marched eight hours northwest through low hills, arrived in plain of Lehélu, but did not reach water; plain surrounded by hills and cultivated. Abyssinian camp about one and a half miles off the spot I am camping in. Shot one *dik-dik*, missed one guinea-fowl with 303. Had a long shot at *gerenook* with 500, missed, went over, I guess, as I could only see top of his back above bush. Saw two day-old pugs of two lions, one with the most enormous foot, bigger than any tiger's I have seen, and far bigger than any lion pug I have yet seen.

14TH, WEDNESDAY.—Moved over to Abyssinian camp in morning, some of them came galloping out to meet me, was taken to their zereba and received by a guard of honour of at least 800 to 850 men. I walked down between two lines of them almost all armed with Remingtons, some with revolvers too; about one in twenty had a muzzle-loader, some had breech-loaders of Vetterli pattern. Was taken to a sort of *darbar* tent and received by the boss, and was told to seat myself on rugs; then we had a long talk through interpreters, two of them, as my speech had to be turned into Somali, and then to Abyssinian, and the boss's into Somali, and then Hindustani. The boss's name (title) is Garadbash Dasili. He was very polite, and had a man behind him with a shield from which hung an enormous black lion's mane. After I left he sent me over two bullocks and three sheep. My tent was full of Abyssinians all day. They are a cheery, manly, very dirty lot. I sent over a large tin of bacon, four bottles of whisky, one *khiali*, four tobes (article of dress), a bag of tobacco, and the Queen's image in Rs. 30. The whisky, bacon and 'baccy were kept, the rest returned. I then went over again and told the boss I was ashamed to take so much and give so little, but he would take no more. I offered him my 303 and 100 rounds. He said I might send him anything through his boss at Harrar when I got back, but he would take nothing now. He heard I wanted donkeys and was trying to buy them, so is going to present me with three to-morrow. Much talk as to whether the Ogaden were British subjects or Abyssinian; my only reply was that I knew nothing political and that this would be settled by Abud, not by me. *Khubber* that two *sahibs* are at Awarra where I am steering for. This stops all my *bundobust* (arrangements). *Khubber* that six lions drink at Fanāt, one march off, very nearly the direction I have come, and that my big-footed friend is one of them. Go to Fanāt to-morrow. Lions probably only three in number at the most, but if, as these people say, they drink regularly in the shallow wells in the river bed, I ought to get some of them. Water here is good; first good water I have had for one month.

15TH, THURSDAY.—My Abyssinian friends came to see me in the morning, so I was a bit late in starting. Fanāt six and three-quarter hours south-south-west in same river. Had a shot at a *gerenouk* with 500, distance 120 yards. He was behind a bush, which I fired through; bullet grazed stump hidden by bush; broke up I fancy, and then hit *gerenouk*, one foreleg broken, very little blood, gave him up after a bit. Men saw a leopard as they were coming along with camels behind me. Pugs (old) of lions at the water here, my large-footed one drank here last night, other pugs about three days. I cannot say how many, but three or four lions appear to drink here occasionally.

16TH, FRIDAY.—No lions came to drink. Went out in morning, but could find no tracks. Met people from *karia*; these say there are four lions, and that they visit their *karia* occasionally, but seldom come on moonlight nights. The lions, they say, drink here about every third day. Made a very cunning ambush in among the roots of a big tree near the water. Will sit up over my ass there to-night. Went out in afternoon; saw two buck *gerenouk*, but could not get a shot. Saw tracks of lesser *koodoo* and a few of *oryx*; some chance of sport here, three small leopards drank here last night.

17TH, SATURDAY.—No lions last night. I went out for a stroll after breakfast after *koodoo*; got back at 2.30, having seen nothing but yesterday's tracks of four lions, one lioness and three cubs I think; wish I had hit them off yesterday, I was close to where I saw them to-day. The big lion appears to have left this; while I was out some men came to the water here, said they had passed Derio (half way between this and Lehēlu) in the early dawn; the big lion was sitting by the wells and growled at them; they remembered that the water at Fanāt was sweeter than at Derio and they left. Just like my luck. About the only day I have been out between 12 and 2 o'clock. Too late to do anything when I heard. The big-footed one is said to have eaten many men of late.

18TH, SUNDAY.—A lion and lioness came last night. There are six paths leading to the water and the least used one of the lot is to leeward of my place; they chose that, got my wind on the bank above me and went off; they roared around a bit and started off towards Derio. Tracked from 6.30 to 12.30, when we found they had been lying under a bush, heard us and gone off. Tracked again till 1.15, when lioness went off in front; I just caught a glimpse of her, but not enough to tell what animal it was. Shikarries did not see her. Tracked her till 1.50, when we heard her go off in thick bush in front. Went back to try for the lion, his pugs led into a thick bit. I stood at the far end, while the other two walked through calling out and making a row; lion broke, but not my way. Gave up, as it was now 2.30 and both lions thoroughly on the look out. Got back to camp 5 p.m., shot two wart hog, right and left, close to camp with 500, distance fifty yards.

19TH, MONDAY.—No lions at night, wild dogs again, they had a grand hunt up the *nullah* (ravine), went off in full cry (jackal's cry mistaken for dogs) like terriers after a cat. Should like to have joined them. My men swear they drove the lions off the other night. I found the skull of a full-grown lioness and a three-quarter grown cub at the water; the people here say they were killed by the dogs. The pack only numbers six, counting three three-quarter grown pups; if they drove off a pair of full-grown lions, how about the "king of beasts"? Went to see my pigs in the morning at 8 a.m.; found a leopard there, missed him disgracefully at sixty yards, standing, and a snap shot in the bush running. Ran ahead to the end of a fringe of thick cover, and came on my leopard at ten yards; he stood sideways and snarled, the little beast; caught him with one of *my* patent express 500 bullets on near shoulder, broke both shoulders, four pieces under skin of opposite shoulder. Male, very dark, spotted skin, much smaller than Indian panther. Moved to Derio. Find the big lion has been drinking here nightly, and the two I was after yesterday drank last night; several pugs of panthers; shall try donkey dodge to-night. Shot a buck *gerenouk*, standing, eighty yards, 303. Hit shoulder, came out behind opposite shoulder. Good horns. Have got into Paget's route, old zereba of his here (last year's); they say he shot two lions here at night, three of my men were with him, they say he killed four lions, his shikarri Abdul

Ashar, four, his brother two, total ten; *all* shot at night, and this is more open country than I have been in yet. Derio, about halfway between Lehēlu and Fanāt.

20th, Tuesday.—At about 12 last night two lions charged across the nullah towards the donkey, gave a snort and vanished. They were to windward, the donkey was eight yards from me, and the place where I was sitting was among some driftwood in the roots of a tree; I had hardly added a stick to it, and you could not see it was artificial in daylight. Neither I nor Jāma moved; I lay still watching the donkey, he faced the lions, snorted and stamped as they came up, and cocked his tail when they ran away; he fully believes he frightened them, but I think Paget must have taught them the donkey trick too thoroughly last year. They are the same two that came at Fanāt. Tracked them into some thick jungle where the ground was too hard for tracking, hunted about in it, but it is a very large bit, and I found nothing. Saw tracks of an ostrich. The big lion did not turn up; he appears to have left the day I arrived, as usual. Went to see if there was anything near the dead *gerenouk*; it has been taken off by men. I thought there was no fear of that, as my men will not eat *gerenouk*. Tracks this morning showed that the lions came up to three yards of the donkey last night.

21st, Wednesday.— No lions; went out in morning to look for tracks, came across a *koudou* (lesser) about a quarter of a mile from camp, standing 125 yards. Shot him with 500 just behind shoulder low down; dropped. Men ran to cut his throat when I saw another buck making off. Called out to the men to stop (as he was going slow), but nothing will stop them when there's a throat to cut. Other *koudou* entered bush, I ran on to head him in direction he was going, could see nothing for some time, and was just thinking of going back to track him when he walked quietly feeding in the bush fifty yards off; had to fire quick because of bushes; going half away, hit in ribs; he disappeared behind bush, and came into view again at about fifty yards, cross shot, going slow and I missed him clean, but he went only about five yards, stood still while I was re-loading, raised his nose in the air and fell, result of first shot. Fired three shots at a *gerenouk* facing me about 100 yards 303 solid, hit him third shot, fair amount of blood at first, soon stopped ; put him up after one hour and-a-half tracking, and he went off strong without giving me a chance ; gave him up. *Koodoo* horns about 24 in., 25 in. straight.

22ND, THURSDAY. — No lions. Started for Fanat in morning. Came across *oryx*, five of them in the bush, got up to about sixty yards. Picked the one that looked the best, he was standing behind a low bush and I could only see his horns and head plainly. Fired through bush, which was thin, and dropped him. Could not get in the next shot till the rest were fully 120 yards off, going like blazes (they were hidden by bush at first), missed, and my *oryx* got up and ran off at a good smart pace, followed track, found him dead about 300 yards on, bullet caught him in middle of body, 500 ex. Buck with good horns, about 34 in. No fresh pugs of lion at Fanat. My big friend was here two out of the three nights I spent at Derio. Shall stay here till he comes back ; he is a wanderer and not a fixture at Derio as I thought.

23RD FRIDAY. — No lions last night. Went

for a stroll east in the morning. Saw *gerenouk*, shot the buck ninety yards, hit him on shoulder a little low, ran about twenty yards and died, 500 ex. Saw more *gerenouk* and tracked a *koodoo* buck for a long way without seeing him. Looked up my *oryx*, found that they had not covered him up properly (I was after the rest while they skinned), and vultures eating him. A good lot left and I had him properly covered. Have two kills to look up to-morrow.

24TH, SATURDAY.—Went out in the morning. No lions here. Had a shot at *gerenouk* buck at about 100 yards, standing straight away from me. Hit him somewhere behind with 500, knocked tids of flesh out, but he went off. Jāma sulked and would not track, for they do not eat *gerenouk*. Lost the *gerenouk*, ground bad, and could find no blood. I think the one I shot left the rest at once and that the tracks we followed were those of the rest. Left Jāma sulking, went on without him. Found men had taken away yesterday, *gerenouk*. Hyæna had visited *oryx*. Found pugs of a large male lion; a new one, I think, tracks led towards water at Derio. Put up a *koodoo* buck as we were following; did not make up my mind, whether to shoot or not, quick enough and lost the chance; followed his tracks a bit, as we were not in ground where lion would lay up. Found tracks of the lion going away from Derio after a drink; followed for about two miles, tracks led on to a low stony hill, where we could carry them no further; beat the hill towards a *nullah*, where there was dense cover; had the lion been on the hill I think he must have come to me. He did not turn up, and I think must have gone on to a thick bit about two miles further, but the ground gave us no chance. He was heading for Fanāt, and I expect him here to-night.

23rd, Sunday.—No lions at Fanāt. People down at the wells half the night. Found tracks of yesterday's lion at Dabino; tracked him to Derio; wells there just stamped with pugs. Moved camp back to Derio again; I ought not to have left it. Pugs led over very stony ground, had Ali only with me, he tracked beautifully, all the way up a long stony valley with hardly a single plain footmark the whole way. Lion went into a range of hills where the best tracker in the world could have done nothing.

We walked quietly about the hill tops looking up likely trees, but there was a very large extent of hill, and I had not the luck to hit off the lion. I think that lion lives in hilly ground, and that he was somewhere on that hill yesterday. I only had three beaters and the hill required twenty to work it, so it is within the bounds of possibility that he broke out round the beat somewhere.

26TH, MONDAY.— No lions. Took a very long stroll looking for tracks, could find none. Missed a *gerenouk* 150 yards, 500 ex.

27TH, TUESDAY.—Man said he had seen rhino pugs in hills about four miles off. Went there, found old pugs, but though we hunted around for a long time we could find no new ones. Saw seven wild dogs on the way, had a long run to try to cut them off in direction they were going, could see none, and gave it up, thinking they had gone ahead, gave rifle to Jāma, and, as I was going back, a big dog jumped out of a bush about three yards off and charged towards me growling; before I could get the rifle he turned and went off through the bush. I had a fairly easy jungle shot at thirty yards, one barrel, and went below him;

the rest of the pack went off. After a run I came up to the last of them standing about 180 yards off. Had a shot at him; bullet went too low; was unsteady for a long shot after a long run.

28th, Wednesday.—No lions. Went to Fanāt, no *khubber* there. Saw two *oryx*; could not get a shot. Saw five *koodoo* does, one *gerenouk* buck; got a shot at him at fifty yards, through thick bush, bullet hit a branch and glanced down on to the ground well short of him. Open a new book to-morrow. I hope with better luck. Man from Gabridari, one march, with *khubber* of five lions, who killed one donkey last night.

SECOND BOOK.

1st March.—Went out, but could find no lion pugs. Saw some *koodoo* does. Went out again in afternoon, shot one *dik-dik*, 303. Missed one, and missed one *gerenouk*, moving, 160 yards. Had a shot at a hyæna running away eighty yards, 303. Picked himself up and went off; followed, found but little blood; gave him up, as it was getting late. Soon after I got back to the tent and while I was tubbing, they said there was a leopard at the wells. I pulled on a pair of trousers and got there as quick as I could, but too late. Followed him up the other bank and got ahead of him, saw him about fifty yards off bolting back through the bush, but as he went straight back towards Ali, who was about thirty yards off, I dare not fire. He turned from Ali, crossed the nullah, lost him in the dark. Hyæna found dead next day by my men.

2ND MARCH, FRIDAY.—No lions. Went out after breakfast, beat all the thick bits round here with seven men. Had a chance at a wild dog, thirty yards, galloping all he knew; went under him both barrels. I cannot shoot running shots with the 500. I could have made certain of hitting him with the paradox (12-bore) had it not come to grief. Saw nothing else. *Khubber* that my big-footed friend has been four nights running to a *karia* beyond Fanāt, at a place called Hador, has killed one donkey, and took a goat out of *zereba* last night. Start for there to-morrow.

3RD MARCH, SATURDAY.—Sat up in *zereba* with donkey. About 2 a.m. was roused out of a comfortable sleep by a rush and much noise. The brave donkey and some animal were on the ground together, but which was which I could not tell. They were only five yards off, but the night was pitch dark and cloudy. I heard only a crunching of bone and sucking of blood. After about five minutes the lioness (for it was a lioness) got up and began trying to drag the donkey backwards. I fired at her shoulder as she was tugging as a terrier pup at a rope, and she dropped. All I heard was a sound as of an animal drawing in breath through a broken windpipe. I thought it was the donkey expiring. After about five minutes of this, the lioness suddenly raised herself on her forelegs. I fired at once as she was nearly out of range of my loophole. Jāma said she lurched back just before I fired and I had missed. I saw nothing when the gun was up. The lioness lay groaning and sucking in her breath about three yards from the *zereba*, but on the side where the drift wood had lodged and I could not see her. I knew then I had hit her in the throat. After about twenty minutes she went slowly off and lay down again about eighty yards off groaning. After about twenty more minutes, all was quiet. At 4.30 I went out of the *zereba*. The donkey had faced the lioness right well, she could not get at his throat, but had seized him across the forehead just above the eyes and had torn the whole front of his head away; he must have died quickly. At 5.30 I started; we followed the tracks for about 200 yards, finding very little blood, when one of the men saw the lioness lying in the open 150 yards off; before I could get the express she was off and went into cover on the river bank. Now I wanted to wait till it was lighter, but all the men were fearfully excited and swore she would be off, &c., and I was persuaded to follow against my judgment. I went down into the *nullah* so as to see better upwards, and Jama very soon made her out about forty yards off, near the top of the bank, in grass under a tree. It was some time before I could make her out; I then saw her head, fired, and she vanished; men said miss; the light was not good enough for a certainty. Followed; after about eighty yards found she had gone into a bush about five yards diameter, covered with dense creeper, so that it was pitch dark inside. I tried to drive her out by standing on one side and making the men fire, but she would not move. Jama and I then went close up and stooped down; he made her out about four yards off, but I could see nothing for a long time, he getting wild with excitement; at last I thought I could make out something yellow where he pointed. I fired and stepped back, expecting a charge. There was a lot of kicking and growling, but no lioness. Soon we went up again and Jama saw her again at five yards; after some time I thought I did, and fired where he pointed, but all was quiet. We went round the other side and Jama saw her head, and said she was dead; after a bit I made it out, and as the nose was in the air and the ears towards the ground, I knew it was right. My first shot at night caught her through the throat just in front of shoulder; second shot her nose off; third (in the morning when she was forty yards off) grazed the top of head, cutting the skin for about one inch; fourth, six inches in front of tail, but a deadly shot, as it was going forward and smashed the spine; fifth, through centre of body; very fat lioness, 7 ft. 10 in. She was one of the pair that nearly got the donkey the other night; the male remained the other side of the nullah, looking on; tracked him into thick jungle close by, too big to beat, and I feared frightening him as usual, so I left him to come and look for his pal to-night. Of course I shall change the *zereba*. *Khubber* from Fanat that the big lion, two lionesses and two small cubs went down to the water there last night, found a woman at the wells, killed and ate her completely, leaving only the feet, and came off in this direction. Expect them to-night, so shall wait here.

4TH MARCH, SUNDAY.—No lions to my dead donkey and lioness. I had the pair dragged to a bush near my *zereba* and sat up in the scent of the slayer and the slain (especially the slain). Nothing came but hyænas by the bushel and a jackal. Moved camp. Started at 5 a.m. Near Dubino came on lion tracks on hard ground. I swore they were fresh (there was just a sprinkle of rain last night at about 3 a.m.), and very fresh; my men both swore they were yesterday's. (I like to record it when I am right, sometimes I forget to put it down when I am wrong.) Went on to the Wells at Durbino and found unmistakable tracks of four lions—one male, one lioness and two cubs, we judged it. Took the tracks back and they went at first towards Derio, whence we had come. After a bit they swerved off the track and then came on to the track again about 400 yards further on, and where we found the pugs on the track they were over our footmarks of the morning, so we had passed each other within about 100 yards, without any knowledge of it on our part; perhaps the lions kept a better look-out. The tracks led on to a long hill above Durbino. We hunted the hill well, getting a track here and there, but found nothing, and the men wanted to give up, as it was impossible to track. Generally I am the one that gives in first, but these lions had eaten that woman at Fanat, and I was extra keen on getting them, so I suggested tracking in a wide sweep all round the hill on the low ground. We found the tracks just as I was going to give it up (in fact, I had made up my mind that if we found no tracks before reaching a tree about 100 yards ahead that I would go back), we came on tracks. We followed them into the usual very high dense grass and bush; after looking up several lively spots we saw the tracks leading to a twenty-foot high tree in thick leaf (fig tree), branches reaching nearly to the ground, and grass up to the branches. It looked good, so we advanced very quietly; Jama looked over the fringe of grass and pointed to the ground, apparently just in front of my feet. I brought up the 10-bore to the "ready," and looked over. As I brought up the gun I touched a branch, and as I looked over the grass I saw something yellow on the ground. It moved as I looked at it, and I was afraid it would run off and be lost

"SHE INSTANTLY THREW THE MOST PERFECT SOMERSAULT."

in the thick grass, so I fired quickly into the middle of it, trusting to weight and lead rather than accuracy, stepped back clear of grass and smoke (Jama going off about five paces to my right) in case of a charge. There was much growling and kicking, and a lioness broke to my left. She crossed a bit of about ten yards of open about twenty yards from me, and I fired the left barrel and rolled her over growling. As I was loading a big beast, looking as big as a full-grown tiger, came from under the fig tree and looked at us. Jama fired my express at it and missed (standing shot ten yards), and it went off towards the open where the other was. I then got two cartridges in and gave her the right barrel, and she instantly threw the most perfect somersault, her tail looked to me to be at least ten feet up in the air. This manœuvre brought her head my way, and she got on her feet and came at me "hell for leather," making much the noise a tiger makes, but not so loud; I think she was quicker in her gallop than a tiger. I had one cartridge and my second gun was nowhere, so I meant to let her come to the muzzle nearly before I loosed. I put up the gun when she was about five yards off and she instantly turned, turned as quick as a flash, her feet cutting great furrows in the ground. I did not fire till I was quite certain she had given it up and then I fired at her hind quarters as she was turning a bush to her left. I felt at the time I had gone to the right of her, loaded and found everything gone. First lioness had picked herself up and gone. They had both gone into dense high grass. I felt certain both were well hit; the one that charged had a big blood splash just behind her shoulder, I saw it as she turned, so I said I would give them an hour to cool; it was half-past 10 o'clock. Jama and Ali got up the tree, but could see nothing. At 11 o'clock I got tired of waiting, and we advanced cautiously into the long grass and found both lionesses lying dead four yards apart, fifteen yards from the small open patch and only about thirty or less from the tree, the grass being so high and dense that neither could be seen from the tree-top. First lioness was evidently lying on her back when I shot her first, for my shot hit her on the elbow and came out at the top of the shoulder, smashing the bone to flinders.

Second shot far back in flank, coming out in centre of body on the other side. The other lioness was shot straight through the body close behind the shoulders. She was an enormous beast, very long, very big-limbed and greyhound-looking about the stomach (all the others I have seen have had big, unwieldy looking stomachs). She is a very old beast apparently, by the teeth. I looked a bit for the cubs while the men were skinning, but lost their tracks in hard ground. On reaching Fanat, and examining the place where the woman was killed, I found only the tracks of the four I saw to-day. They put down the lioness as a big lion (she has a fine foot for a number nine shoe). I am really content with getting these beasts, and preventing further manslaughter on their part. When I got to Fanat, 3.15 p.m., *khubber* that the big lion I tracked into the hills two days ago, went to a *Karia* beyond Hador the night before last, took out a woman and eat her. It was a *Midgan Karia*, and they tracked him and fired a poisoned arrow into him. Nine *Midgans* went after him to-day. Found he had gone into dense grass, after having been very sick, and they were afraid to follow. Shall go

there to-morrow. They have sent a man to show
me the way. Must not forget to record Ali's
behaviour when the big lioness charged. He was
standing close to me with nothing but my rhino-
hide whip in his hands, and he moved not an
inch. That's what I reckon is the highest class
of courage. It looked like a charge home; in fact,
the distance from my footmarks to the nearest
furrow of her feet when she turned was less than
four yards. Had I killed her at six yards it
would have been a clear case of a lioness charg-
ing home.

5TH MARCH, MONDAY.—*The* big lion came down
to water at Fanat last night, came past my zereba
without even having a look at the camels or the
donkey tied outside, and it was a pitch-dark
night with a little rain. I could not understand
it, I did not follow his tracks, as I wanted to get
the one wounded by the *Midgans*. I went to
their *karia*, about one hour's march. They told
me they had heard the lion leap into the zereba,
and some men ran out to protect their cattle.
The lion entered one of the huts, seized a woman,
threw her over the fence and jumped after her,
and was off with her into the jungle before they

could do anything. They tracked him next morning and put him up, firing some arrows at him, one of which they said hit him in the side; the arrow had a little poison on. I found the lion had lain down in several places, and had been sick several times, and I was certain it was *the* big one. Presently we found this morning's track leading out of the dense bit, and we took it straight back to my camp. We got back at twelve o'clock with all the morning wasted. I was dead tired, for I had sat up over the tied donkey again last night. We tracked him through fairly thin jungle with occasional thick bits (very small ones), the first thick bit that his tracks led into. Jama got up a tree to see if he could make him out; he saw him about 150 yards off sneaking away; said he was an enormous beast, very dark, without much mane. He was evidently very wide awake, as we had come quietly. After having repeated this performance to two more thick bits, the next one we came to I went quietly on ahead, round by the right, but he was too smart and broke out to the left. Then a heavy thunder-shower came on and washed out tracks, so we gave up. I am afraid the *Midgans* have frightened him too much for me to get him. It is a nuisance, as they all say he has killed a lot of people lately. The ones I killed were his family party, but were not with him when he killed the *Midgan* woman, for that was the night they killed a woman at Fanat. By-the-bye, those lionesses measure 7 ft. 8 in. and 8 ft. 2 in. Heavy showers all the afternoon, and it looks like a wet night.

6TH MARCH, TUESDAY.—Could find no traces of big lion this morning. He must have gone off some way before the heavy showers of yesterday afternoon. Went towards Dubino to see if he had gone there; no tracks. Looked up my dead lionesses—found the cubs had dragged off the fat one and eaten of it. A heavy storm of rain just before I got there spoilt the tracking, and I could not make out where they had gone. Missed a *gerenouk*, twelve yards, trotting, 500 ex-bullet, went low.

7TH MARCH, WEDNESDAY.—Went out looking for tracks. Took a long round, as far as Derio, and could find none. The ground is very hard after the rain, and it was easy to pass tracks without seeing them. Had a shot at a *gerenouk* at 100 yards after a very patient stalk. I was spotted by the does, and had to sit still for about twenty minutes. Shot him in front of shoulder, facing me, 500 ex. Horns indifferent. Had a shot at another, 180 yards, went high. Almost all of my cartridges for 500 are loaded with a batch of rank bad powder. Shoots very low, little recoil, and the bullet does not break up fairly in a beast.

8TH MARCH, THURSDAY.—Marched for Lehelu. Went to look up yesterday's *gerenouk*, found it gone. Men's tracks; took them up and came on Ahmed and another in the act of cutting it up. As Ahmed (the head man of the Dubino *karair* has had many presents from me, and as I had especially warned him about removing my game I was angry. He was wearing a brand new tobe I had given him and a spear. I took both, and left him to return in Garden of Eden dress. Went out on Lehelu plain in the evening after a head of *aoul*. The Abyssinians had made them very wary. However, I got a shot at about 250 yards with 303, and hit a doe in the neck. It *was* the one I aimed at. I could not tell her from a buck. Horns 13 inches. Missed a *gerenouk* 500 ex., running (100 yards), in bush.

9TH MARCH, FRIDAY.—Went out after *aoul* in the morning. Saw a herd of about ten, near a nullah, and told my men to walk round them so as to make them move towards the nullah. This being a new form of circumventing antelope to the Somali shikaries, they would not believe it could work, so they went about 200 yards and sat down behind a bush, leaving the *aoul* to feed about at their own sweet will. After lying on my stomach in the sun for about three-quarters of an hour, I concluded something was wrong and tried a long shot, 300 yards sight, 303, taking it fairly full, went over; buck did not know where the shot came from (smokeless powder) and stood still; took a fine sight, aimed low and hit him or grazed him in the stomach, I think; fired four more shots at various distances up to 400 yards without hitting him again; followed him a long way across the open plain but could not get near, and as he did not seem a bit the worse I gave it up. Marched in the afternoon for two and three-quarter hours, nearly north, just a little west. A starving Somali boy who has been hanging round my camp for some days getting what he could, followed me. I was inclined to send him back, owing to the difficulties of water (for I shall probably get none for seven days), but hearing his tale I pitied him and took him on as extra donkey boy. I must wash less, that is all! I have now twenty-two in all, instead of nineteen as before. Abdilleh (head man) has taken unto himself a wife. The ceremony, as far as I could see, consisted in bringing her into my camp after having borrowed an advance from me for payment. He says the thing has been on since last year, when his father sent down four ponies and five camels for her. I should reckon her dear at the price, judging from looks, but there may be good in her that does not appear to the eye. Another Abdilleh (a *mullah*) has attached himself to me as guide, not that I want him much, and now Yusuf, the starving boy, is brought on the strength. When the Abyssinians raided this country last year for the first time, they shot almost all the men of his *karia;* his father is dead, and his mother is wandering around with three smaller children picking up what food she can.

10TH MARCH, SATURDAY.—Marched at 5 a.m. General direction a little east of north. Country low hills and thin bush with open places. At 8.30 one of the men came running up (I was well in advance of the camels) to say that I had taken the wrong road. I could hardly believe it, as I was evidently, from the camel droppings, on a *gafila* track and my direction was about right for Luckhu. However, he said Abdilleh had sent him on; I concluded it was Abdilleh the guide and not Abdilleh the head man, who knew no more of the country than I did. I would not leave the track until he said he had actually seen my camels take another road to the right. I struck off to the right then, across the hills, and went on without finding another road till I came to the foot of a higher range, over which I was sure the road did not go, so back I went till I heard a shot, and at 11.55 arrived at the place my camels reached at about 10 o'clock on the very track I had left, and but a short half-hour's walk from where I had left it. My camels had gone wrong and come back into the right road. Abdilleh the head man had let Abdilleh the guide fall behind the camels and had taken on himself the guiding of them. I had three hours' needless hard walking in consequence. Shot a *gerenouk*,

200 yards, hit him high in the neck (he was facing me), using the 200 sight with riflcite in the 303. I ought to have used the 100 sight. Missed another (fired over him) at about 250, using 200 sight full. Saw two *oryx* in the evening but could not get a shot. Marched for two and three-quarter hours in afternoon; total, deducting the march on the wrong road, about seven hours.

11TH MARCH, SUNDAY.—Shot disgracefully to-day. In the early morning just as the sun was setting up I saw a herd of about fifteen *oryx*. All the *oryx* I have yet seen have been very wild; this was a tame herd, only I did not know it. I could only get to about 200 yards and then the ground was very open, and I dared not try to get nearer. The light was very bad, but I could not wait, as they were feeding away from me into an open maidan. Used 303, first shot miss, second hit, heard crack of bullet plainly, third shot running, a good 250 yards, hit, brought the buck (and he was a big one) on to his head, but he got up and went off. After running some way, I got another long moving shot and hit again, then two misses, then I ran up a low hill after the herd and came on them all at about eighty yards. Missed clean with 303, and fired both barrels of the express at the buck, missing him again twice; ran after him in thick bush and got a standing shot at about sixty yards the other side of the buck and missed again. All had now gone; I had, I believe, hit three separate big bucks. The one that fell left the herd, and as he appeared very big and the worst hit I took him first; followed his blood track till 8.30. From the height of the blood marks on the grass (about three inches above my knee) he must have been hit low on the shoulder. His track took me at right angles from the road and away from the line of the rest of the herd. I gave him up, as I had to catch up the *gafila*, and I had to give up the others too. The worst of this shooting on the march is the losing of wounded animals. I should probably have been able to follow him to the death and should have found one if not both the others (I think they were badly hit, I saw a good deal of blood on the track of the herd where I crossed it) had I been halted. Did not get to the camp till 11.30, walking very fast. Started at 4 o'clock, marched till 10, and again from 3 to

5 o'clock. Met a *gafila*; they said there is plenty of water at Luckhu. Saw a buck of Clarke's gazelle in the afternoon, but could not get a shot. Killed a *dik-dik* for dinner, forty yards.

12TH MARCH, MONDAY.—Reached Garhati at 7 a.m. Tank nearly full of water, and wells full of rain water and insects. Lot of sheldrake on the tank. Shot two sheldrake, one guinea-fowl, eight *dik-dik*, and lost three wounded *dik-dik*. Fired exactly twenty rounds solid bullet 303. Shooting rather good, as *dik-dik* were wild. Green grass all over the place. Camels, horse, donkeys and goats gorging to repletion. Camels came in the evening romping into the zereba and looking like animated *mussacks*. Moved on to Luckhu at noon. Plenty of rain water in the wells, and two tanks there. No *karias* here.

13TH MARCH, TUESDAY.—Started at 5 a.m., marched till 10, and again from 2 to 5 p.m. Saw a herd of about fifteen *oryx*. Could not get cover nearer than 200 yards. Used 303, fired five shots, first shot hit, second hit, both big bucks, third, fourth, and fifth shots at about 300 yards, fifth hit. Found two blood tracks, one with very little and one with plenty of blood. Followed for

a long way, blood stopped and I had to give it
up. Saw some *aoul* near where we halted for the
morning in a very open plain, had one shot at
303 yards, missed. Got to breakfast at 12
o'clock. Started out again at 1 p.m. after the
aoul, got one shot with 200 *full* sight, *aoul* fell,
but picked himself up and went off slowly for
about half a mile. Watched him with glasses—
he stood for about twenty minutes but would not
lie down. Jàma spotted two *oryx* in the direction we had to go, the wounded *aoul* having gone
in the opposite direction. I left him, stalked the
oryx, and got within about eighty yards of a good
buck. I fired over long grass under the branches
of a bush, the smoke hung and I could not see
effect (using 500 ex.). When smoke cleared *oryx*
was standing in same spot apparently untouched;
thought I had gone low; used fuller sight, *oryx*
ran about ten yards and looked about; fired again
and saw that the bullet cut a branch over his
back. *Oryx* went off at a good pace, took up
303 and fired as he ran. Heard bullet hit, followed, not much blood. Found *oryx* under a
bush about 400 yards on, dying. First shot (I
think) caught him in centre of body high up,

next two shots over. The shot with 303, Jeffery bullet, caught him in the ribs and passed through like a solid bullet without breaking. Horns thirty-one inches. The 303 is not good enough for *oryx* and I must give it up. Saw lion pugs about six days old in the Ahamati bush jungle. Had a shot at a *gerenouk*, 200 yards. Heard bullet hit, and as he stood quite still looking at the spot where the bullet struck the sand (for it passed through), I got behind a bush and managed to get 100 yards nearer, when he saw me and faced my way. Fired again, caught him in centre of chest and dropped him; first shot through foreleg grazing chest. Another buck ran off, followed him and got a shot at about 120 yards. Hit him on centre of shoulder, bullet passed through both shoulders, and he ran on a bit (only one shoulder broken) and fell dead. The Jeffery bullet is very uncertain as to whether it breaks up or not.

14TH MARCH, WEDNESDAY.—Marched 5 a.m. Camels reached Darur at 11 a.m. Found tank full of water, nice clean water, too. No *Karias* ever come here, as it is on the boundary between the Habr Unis and Ogaden country; only *kafilas* pass through; rocky, sandy soil all round. This is the first good drinking water I have tasted since I left Berbera. Saw a herd of *oryx* on the way. Could not get near, and would not take a long shot. Had a shot at a *gerenouk* 200 yards, fired standing, 303, bullet passed through both shoulders. Went for a stroll in evening; saw an *oryx* close to camp. He was looking at something else and snorting, and bolted just as I had got up to about 180 yards and was getting the sights nicely on him; too much bush for a running shot, left him for another day and went to see what had frightened him, hoping it was a lion. Inspected a bit of thick bush, nothing there. Then I caught sight of something yellow, about the size of a lion's head, creeping through the grass towards us about fifty yards off. Jama looked at it for a bit and then laughed much. It was a huge land-tortoise; its great big hump-backed shell was bigger than a lion's head and much the same colour.

15TH MARCH, THURSDAY.—Went out in morning, saw a herd of *oryx*, ground too open, could not get near. Saw a very big single buck on way back. Fired three shots at him galloping through thin bush about 100 yards (he came all round me) with the 500, all misses. Went out in evening, saw nothing.

16TH MARCH, FRIDAY.—Moved camp about three miles north of Darur to the place where I saw fresh lion pugs on the march down. Went out in morning. Saw the single *oryx* I missed yesterday, but he saw me first and went off from the maidan into bush. I expected him to go some way and entered the bush rather carelessly. Oryx was near the edge of it, spotted me, and went off again. This time I had to follow his tracks about one mile before I saw him. Stalked him successfully up to about eighty yards; he saw me as I raised the rifle and stood turned partly toward me. Shot grazed point of shoulder, entering body just behind it. He turned, went about five yards, and stood looking at his side. Caught him in middle of body with left barrel; he went off and stood again at about 120 yards. Caught him in centre of body high up and dropped him. When we got to him he stood up and faced us with his head lowered. The Somalis tell me an *oryx* is not at all a safe beast to cut the throat of if a bit lively. I gave him one more bullet to settle the business and he fell nearly dead. The 500 with Eley bullet is not good enough for a powerful beast like an *oryx*. Horns thirty-two inches. Went out in afternoon, saw several Clarke's gazelles, but only as they ran through jungle. Do not know if a buck was among them. Saw doe of lesser *koodoo*. Saw three *oryx*, all looked good heads (with glasses); got up to 100 to 120 yards, fired at biggest looking beast. I could only see their heads and top of their backs over the grass as I stood. First shot evidently hit, and apparently *oryx* regularly staggered by it, the rest did not move at the shot. Fired at the next best, and he blundered around as if he was dying; the remaining one went off unharmed. Before I had loaded again the second *oryx* had vanished in the grass, but the first I fired at still stood. I fired at him again and heard the bullet singing across country, low, I think; he went off and I missed him again, left barrel; ran after him with 10-bore and fired another shot at him in thick bush, missed again. Followed him till about 4.30 (two hours) very little blood, only a drop or two in every hundred yards. Got a shot at him at about 150 yards at 4.30

p.m., missed again, low as usual. He now began to fail, I could see from his tracks, and at about 4.50 I came up to him again, about 130 yards, standing in high grass; hit him in centre of body and he fell. When I looked at him I found my first bullet had been exactly correctly placed, in the very centre of the shoulder, but very little damage was done except smashing the shoulder. Another bullet had just touched the bottom of his chest, close behind the forearm. Horns

Had no time to look up the other wounded one. Must not fire at a second beast again till the first is actually on the ground.

17TH MARCH, SATURDAY. — Went out in the morning, took a long round, getting back at 1 p.m. Saw only two *oryx*, female and *butcha* (young one). Fired at a buck Clarke's gazelle, at about 250 yards. I had no hope of getting nearer, as the ground was open, and he had seen me. Used 500 ex., bullet went low. Saw two more and got up to about 150 yards, both does. Saw doe *koodoo*. As I was coming back I saw two of my camel men with two prisoners; two spies of the Habr Unis had come down to find out if any Ogaden *karias* were out. They saw my camels and took them for Ogaden, and they were lying behind a bush watching for a chance to steal one or two. My men had kept a better look out and spotted the strangers, got round behind them, so that they were between my camels and my *zereba* (which was about half a mile off) and the two stalkers; they got right up to them, then put up their carbines and said they would shoot if the men moved, took them prisoners, collared their spears, and brought them in. They were known to some of my men (I have ten Habr Unis with me), in fact, they belong to the same *karia* as Karshia, one of my lot. There was no doubt that they would not have touched the camels had they known them to belong to a Sahib, so their spears were returned and they are now feasting with my lot. They tell me all the Habr Unis braves are on the war path about two marches off, and that there has been much rain further on, but not enough for me to find water. As I write, an alarm—men seen on road close to *zereba*. My men went out after them with a rush. They recognised Karshia's voice and called out to him by name. More Habr Unis on the look out for Ogaden—eight of them. One has to take note of passers-by in this uninhabited spot, for they are generally on the loot when far from their *karias*. My men told the Habr Unis where the Ogaden *karias* are, and they went off after them

18TH MARCH.—The Habr Unis men told me they saw fresh tracks of a rhino about two hours from here, so I went that way in the morning. Came on the yesterday's track in about two hours and followed it in the hope that I should find his dwelling place. No good. That rhino was moving to better grazing; he went in a bee line straight away from my camp. No rain has fallen in that direction, and all the grass is dry, so I guess he was moving across the dry patch. He was not feeding as he went, which is a very bad sign. The dry bit extends for about thirty-five miles, so the Habr Unis men said. I gave up the business after about two and a-half hours' fast tracking, and it took me four hours' good walking to get back. Was quite done. Get no milk here, and Warsama's cooking is beginning to choke me off my feed. Am getting very thin and weak. If I could get milk I could do well. I drank about a gallon a day in the Ogaden country, and miss it badly here. Jāma cracked my express across the stock. He is doing me well with my guns. Broken striker of my pet 12-bore on Jan. 22, and I have missed that gun every day since. Broke off one of the indicators of my express about ten days later, and now he has cracked the stock. These men treat guns as if you could cut a new one off any tree.

19TH MARCH, MONDAY.—Felt seedy, so sat tight and sent men in two directions for *khubber*. Nothing. They never see anything unless I am with them. Spent all the day in making a new sight for my 500, out of an *oryx* bone. Made a very good one considering that I had no tools but a blunt knife. They have lost both my files. Went out for a bit before breakfast because one of the camel men said he had seen three *oryx* close by. I do not believe him, as he could neither show me the beasts or their fresh tracks. Plenty of stale ones, and I believe he took me out on spec, having seen these.

20TH MARCH, TUESDAY.—Went out at 7.30 and fooled around till 11.30, saw no tracks of anything good. Saw one very good buck *oryx*, and made a mess of the stalk through being in too much of a hurry; followed him up but could not come near him again. Camels left camp at 2 o'clock and marched till 4.45.

21st March, Wednesday.—A little luck to-day. Met all the Habr Unis camels in the morning going in batches to Darur for water; track nothing but men and camels; expected to see nothing. At about 5.45, I spotted a rhino strolling along about 300 yards ahead in very open ground, a perfect *maidan* plain, with a few scattered low bushes. The wind was blowing from us almost dead down the road, and my only chance was to rush him before he crossed the road and got our wind. I could not get there quick enough, for though the rhino has bad sight one cannot quite run at him in the open. When I was running to cross his front, under what cover a three-foot bush some fifty yards ahead gave me, he stopped, raised his nose in the air towards the road where my men were lying, turned round and lumbered off the way he had come (I was about 150 yards from him then); I knew he had seen no one, and had hopes he would not go far. After about 300 yards he broke into a walk. Jama and I followed him about 500 yards behind, keeping under any cover we could see and well to leeward. This went on for about a mile, and he was circling back towards the track again, when I saw, half a mile ahead of him, a string of camels coming down the road. We doubled all we knew, almost in the bare open, only taking heed of the wind, to get to him before he saw the camels. I got up to about eighty yards, panting like a steam engine, just as he saw the camels. He stood side on to me, a little turned away, with his head well away from me, looking at the camels. I could trust the 10-bore this distance, so I took him a little behind the shoulder (shoulder shot no use from his position) and held it as steady as my run would let me. I did not see the effect as the smoke came back in my face, but Jama said "lagga" (hit). I heard two snorts, saw the rhino turn partly my way, put his nose down so that his horn almost touched the ground, and come tearing along at a very smart pace. After about thirty yards his nose went up to normal position, and he passed some fifty yards to my right. I kept the left barrel till he was level with me and fired just in front of his nose. He was going faster than I thought, for the bullet caught him far back and high on the stomach. Down went his nose again and he did another little charge, passing about forty yards to my right rear. He went for about 150 yards, stopped, staggered and fell. When I got up to him he was not dead, so I gave him one in the neck, towards the brain, which killed him. The men say he is a very big male, and that his horn is the biggest they have seen. Jāma says it measures about two inches more than Wood's best, which was considered very good. Measurements—front horn 19 in. long, 21 in. circumference; rear horn 8½ in. long. A much bigger beast than the cow rhino I shot. I believe he would have charged if he had seen me, but I cannot say. If the rhino charges as that one went, with his head right down, then the tales about the difficulty of stopping a rhino charge must be rot. The whole of the upper part of the neck and the spine between the shoulders must be open to a shot, and what better place could you wish for to stop a beast. First bullet six inches behind right shoulder, under skin on opposite shoulder blade, but bone not broken. Second shot, through stomach high up, under skin on opposite side. N.B.—Both bullet holes closed up by skin, *no blood* except that snorted out of nose. Shot an *oryx*, female, head 28 in., only one I saw. Meat badly wanted, or I would have let her alone. I have had nothing but *chupatties* (flat unleavened cakes) for two days. Distance 120 yards, 500 ex., turned slightly away, hit in loins and dropped on spot. Had shot two *dik-dik* before out of three shots, but two *dik-dik* will not feed my crowd. Found a Somali woman, she had lost the party she was with, who were going to Darur, and she was badly athirst, going to lie down under a bush and wait for them to come back. Meanwhile, the lions would probably have got her, for I have seen plenty of old tracks to-day, and some are certain to go down the road one way or another after the camels. Gave the woman food and water, and made her come with my party back towards her *karia*, which we shall reach to-morrow morning. Tracks of lions all about the spot I am camped in, about two days old. Marched from four to ten o'clock and about three hours in afternoon. Can keep time no longer for my watch has stuck work.

Diary.

22ND MARCH, THURSDAY.—Fever last night, only got to sleep about 12.30, and they started loading up at 2.45 instead of 3.15, as I had ordered. Marched about one and a-half hours along the road and two and a-half west to near some *karias* (Gerōdi). Fever came on again about 8 a.m., and I felt much knocked up. Jama saw tracks of lioness and two cubs near the camp. I started at 10; beautiful open jungle with a few scattered bushes, but the tracking was hard, owing to the surface being hardened by recent rain. Lost tracks at 12 and I gave up. Had I been fit I would have sent for more men and kept on, and would probably have got the lioness. (Ibraham Yei, Habr Unis, will show shikar in this direction).

23RD MARCH, FRIDAY.—Marched from 4.30 to 10.30 and from 3 to 6 o'clock. Got well into Thoio plain. Large herds of *aoul* there, absolutely unapproachable, and my men could not drive them. It is no use telling them that to go a long round and advance straight on to the antelope is the wrong way; they will not do the proper trick of edging round close to the antelope and making them circle gradually your way.

After failing to drive I tried some long range shots at two solitary bucks, one 300 yards sight (fell short), three at 400 yards, two at 500 yards, all misses, could not get correct elevation. Have shut up the 10-bore; lion country left behind. Can see Gan Libah from here and feel quite close to Berbera. Any amount of *karias* going out into the Haud now. This is the time I ought to have begun my shoot. Had I started on 1st April from Berbera, I think I could have made a bag of lions.

24TH MARCH, SATURDAY.—Marched from 4 to 10.40 and from 3 to 6. Got nearly as far as Oonoonoof, shall be able to get to Asa to-morrow afternoon. I hear there is good grazing there, and I can have another try for *koodoo* on 26th, giving the camels a day for rest and feed; they got no grazing to-day, the country is bare after Thoio. Saw no game except *gerenouk* to-day, and I have shot enough of them. Had one shot at a guinea-fowl about seventy yards, 303, killed.

25TH MARCH, SUNDAY.—Marched into Syk in the morning, and on to Jaretta in the evening. I left the camels and went to look for *aoul* in the plain near Oonoonoof. Found about fifteen tolerably near some bushes. Got up to about 180 yards. Took a very good buck, shot him in shoulder, dropped. Fired at another buck moving 200 yards, and over. Fluked him through the head, smashing all the bones so that the horns hung limp. Fired at a third, the last in the herd, as the one that moves off last is generally a buck (and I could not tell bucks from does at the distance); I used 300 sight full. First shot over, did not move, took 300 fine and hit him; followed for about a mile, firing occasional long shots at him in the open plain. He got into some thin bush and I got up to 120 yards. First shot not a move, second shot put his head down; third shot dropped, both forelegs broken at elbow; finished him with a shot through the shoulder at a short range. I had no knife and my men were skinning the others. Found first bullet had hit her (for it was a doe) through the thigh, passing into the stomach; one shot grazed thigh, one passed through ribs without breaking, one passed through ribs tearing a big hole the other side, one broke both forelegs and then the finisher; six hits out of nine shots fired at her. Saw a wart hog standing facing me eighty yards. Hit dead centre between the eyes, killed him dead. In the afternoon had a shot fired from standing position at a gazelle, 170 yards. Hit him just in front of shoulder, passing out of other shoulder, dropped, a very good shot (or a fluke) for so small a mark. Had a shot at an *aoul*, 130 yards, knew it was a doe, but I wanted a head skin for one of the bucks. I shot, hit through spine far back, dropped. Very old doe, with a very good head and skin; altogether the shooting to-day was much beyond my average, but the 303 is not powerful enough unless you can get so close as to put your bullet exactly right. Heads, *aoul* bucks 18 in. and $15\frac{1}{2}$ in.; does 15 in. and $13\frac{1}{2}$ in.; gazelle $12\frac{1}{2}$ in. Saved a life to make up for this slaughter. Found a little boy dying of hunger and thirst on the Haud. Gave him water, had him brought on a camel and gave him some strong *aoul* soup with cornflour in it. This revived the little skeleton enough to let him talk. His name is Ismail, and he comes from the Abasgul Ogaden. Abyssinians killed his father, his mother died and he has been wandering round, following *gafilas* since. Says he does not know how long he has been lying near the road, but an Eda Galla *gafila* passed him four days ago, and gave him no food or drink. He got quite cheery and wanted to walk this evening, but he was mounted between two of my portmanteaux on a camel. Have just seen that he has had another cupful of soup and a little rice, and tucked him up comfortably. He wants more to eat, he says, but I do not think it good for him.

26TH MARCH, MONDAY.—Started at 6.30 after a feed, taking a half *chupatti* in my pocket. Walked till 11.30 on the hills, seeing only five doe *koodoo* and seven *alikut*, none of which I wanted. Started on the backward trail at 12.30, and at 2 p.m. came on a buck. He had my wind and was going fairly fast through bush at about 200 yards. I was well above him and could see well. I fired four cartridges, the third of which hit him, followed him and put him up again about 3 o'clock, not much blood up till then. Had a very snap shot at his stern at thirty yards, hit, I am certain, for we now found much more blood, and blood on the bushes on both sides of him instead of one. Followed till 5.15, when I ordered to give up, as the ground was too bad to walk in after dark. We got back at 6.30, after an hour and a-half of very fast going over hills, eleven hours footing it in pretty stiff ground; once was taken to the very bottom of the Golis range by the wounded beast, and up to the top again before we left him.

27TH MARCH, TUESDAY.—Sent Jāma and Ali to look if wounded *koodoo* was dead; they said he had gone up to Gan Libah, where they did not follow (no time). I walked along the hills and down to Mandera, saw plenty of fresh *koodoo* tracks but no *koodoo*. On to Leferug in the afternoon. News—hear that the Habr Unis strength is about 150; were close to me when I was at Darur, and that one of their spies found my camp. (My men saw his tracks, but we thought it was one of the Ogaden come to see if there was water at Darur.) These men, probably joined by the eight who came to me, went on to Handiget and hung around, waiting for the Ogaden. Rer Harun Ogaden came up strong, ten *karias* and lots of camels. Habr Unis attacked them before they had made *zerebas*, and made a big bag, men, women, and children. They only lost three men killed in the fight, and brought back between 450 and 500 camels. All the men had three camels each for their share, besides the amount for the bosses. My Habr Unis men are very cheery over it, for the Rer Harun are their biggest enemies and killed the chief of their section (Sultan Nur's section) of the Habr Unis last year. They say that nearly 100 (counting cubs) of the Ogaden, were killed, but this, like all despatches, is probably nearly true when divided by three.

28TH MARCH, WEDNESDAY.—Marched to Dera Godli in the morning. After breakfast Hassan came to say he had seen an *aoul* buck close by. Stalked him in good ground, got to eighty yards, and shot him just behind shoulder. Bullet came out other side just in front of hip (303 Jeffery). Marched to Nasia in afternoon; saw another good buck *aoul*, had to run up a slope as he was moving off; got an easy standing shot, eighty yards (fired standing), and made a miss over his back, and missed him again at about 350 yards. People here say Abyssinians have attacked Lord Delamere's party and killed some of his men. Wonder if it was Dasali's party on their way back.

Here the diaries end abruptly and no further particulars are given of the return to Aden. Doubtless Captain Francis's shooting came to end at this point and the diaries were only written to recount the actual sport.

Extract from an Indian Newspaper, in May, 1894.

"The death of Captain John Cyril Francis, of the 5th Bombay Infantry, who fell a victim to cholera at Deolali on the 4th of May, at thirty-eight years of age, will be sincerely mourned by a very large number of people on the Bombay side.

"A smart officer, a keen sportsman and a kind-hearted, genial, courteous gentleman, poor "Jack Francis" was popular wherever he went. He was beloved by all ranks in his regiment, and every officer who enjoyed the privilege of being one of his pupils at the Deolali Musketry Class, can bear testimony to the zeal and tact with which he discharged the somewhat trying duties of an instructor at that institution. For the last two years Captain Francis had held the appointment of D.A.A.G. for Musketry, 2nd Circle, a berth for which he was singularly well qualified; as, in addition to his natural advantages of temper and manner, he was an excellent shot with the rifle, and the best revolver shot in India.

"Captain Francis served in Afghanistan and in Egypt, and was present at the actions of Hashon, Tofrik and Tamai. He only lately returned from a shooting expedition in Somali Land, and but for being much reduced after three months' hard work on poor fare, was in excellent health when he returned, about a fortnight ago, to Deolali, to prepare for the commencement of the School of Musketry course.

"He bore his short but painful illness with the same pluck with which he had ever faced trouble and danger throughout his life, and at one time there were hopes that he would rally, but on the fourth day he sank, and at 3 a.m. on Friday, the 4th, he died."

NOTES ON THE WAHALI GAFILA ROUTE.

1st March.—Berbera to Dera Godli, twenty-four miles, water, south-west.

2nd March.—Dera Godli to Leferug, thirteen miles, water, south-west.

3rd March.—Leferug to Maudera, ten miles, water, south-west.

4th March.—Maudera to Adalch, fifteen miles, water, road south, passes through Assa Range. Pass easy for laden camels. Water obtainable at Jaretta at head of pass, also at Syk, pass easy for laden camels.

5th March. — Adalch twenty-five miles, no water. For first three miles road passes through undulating ground with low stony hills. It then enters an open plain with here and there a few bushes; the bush increases after passing Oonoonoof (twelve miles), a long hill about 300 feet high, one and a-half miles to left of road. After Oonoonoof a level plain with mimosa. Then scattered bush-jungle, bushes about sixty yards apart with occasional more open patches. Broad, firm, sandy track, easy going; good camel grazing through most of the year; grass on plain between Adaleh and Oonoonoof, south.

6TH MARCH.—Twenty-five miles. After about seven miles the road enters an open plain called Thoio, about eighteen miles across from north to south, and stretching to the horizon east and west. Plain covered with grass all the year round. No water. Halt south end of plain.

7TH MARCH.—After leaving Thoio, road enters bush-jungle similar to that between Oonoonoof and Thoio. Halt at about twenty-five miles near Garodi which lies about three miles west. Good grazing for camels, and fair grass for horses. No water, south.

8TH MARCH.—Bush gradually gets thinner and road passes through several large open spaces. Halt twenty-five miles in open plain called Bibel; good grass, no water, south.

9TH MARCH.—Road passes through alternate patches of dense bush and open plain, grass higher and bush patches denser than before. At twenty-four miles enters slightly undulating ground with black stones; twenty-five miles, Darur, a natural depression, said by some Somalis to have been artificially deepened by a race which inhabited the country before the Somalis. These depressions are called *harro* and the men report three similar ones from one to two days to the East.

In January the *harro* was dry; in March it was a long stretch of water 400 by 200 feet, about waist deep in centre. No wells have been dug here apparently because it is the border line between the Habr Unis and Ogaden, and in consequence of intertribal raids, *karias* seldom camp near it. A well giving permanent water could be dug at a small cost, good grass and camel grazing.

10TH MARCH. — Twenty-five miles, south. Track passes through dense bush and high grass with occasional open patches. At Ahamali very dense thorn bush strip about four miles wide. Road very winding on account of bush, no grass in this patch; ground undulating, good grazing in plain.

11TH MARCH. — Ahamali, across undulating, open ground covered with grass; said to be water here throughout the rains. Lackhu reached about sixteenth mile, halt. Two *harro* with five wells in one and four in the other. Little water in the wells in January, enough to fill casks. I was able to obtain about 250 gallons. Gurhati similar. Harro with wells about three miles, south-west (dig). Same three miles further west. (All the country round here contains depressions which hold water in rains.) From here there are two *gafila* routes, the most used one is that to Lehelu. In March, all wells were full and the *harros* half-filled with water. Eight to ten *karias* were getting water from the district in January. All had left except one *karia* of Midgans when, I returned in March. The water was reported to have been insufficient and the *karias* moved towards Lehelu in February. The people said it was a bad year for water. Lehelu about sixty miles south, south-west. First march through similar ground to that around Lakhu. Second march passes through low hills, road gradually descending all the way till the plain of Lehelu is reached. Lehelu cultivated valley, water obtainable in shallow wells in bed of river running through valley to south-east. Jowari cultivation. Also cultivation at Warandab on other side of river. Second route, south-east.

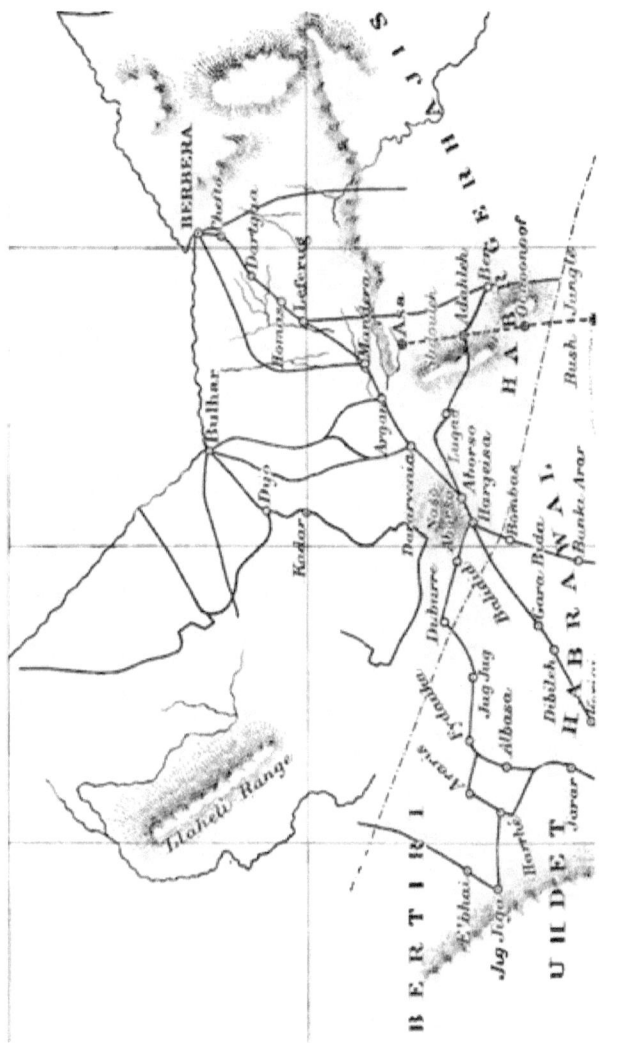

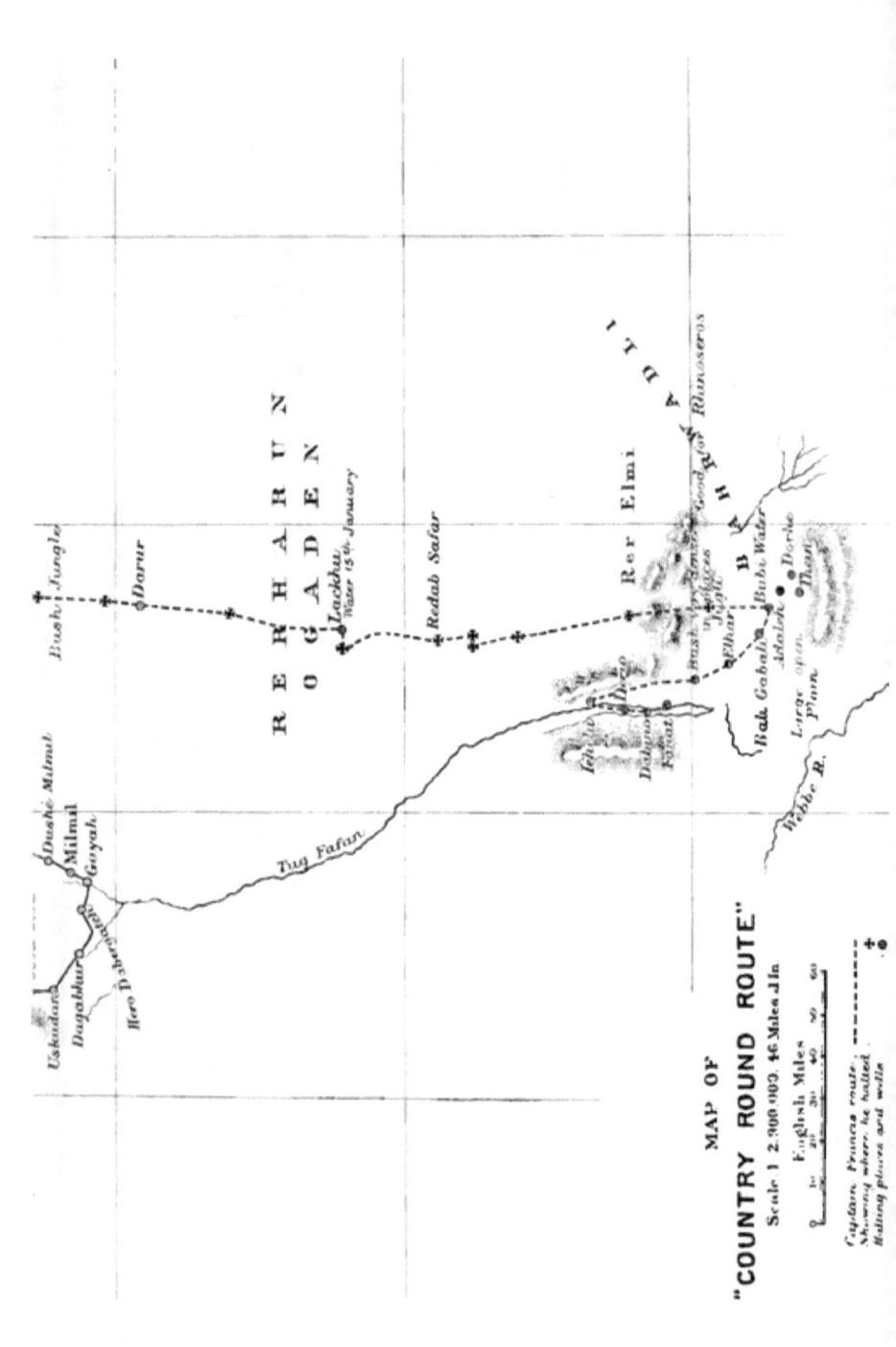

www.ingramcontent.com/pod-product-compliance
Lightning Source LLC
Chambersburg PA
CBHW030410170426
43202CB00010B/1555